ANSEL
Engagement Calendar 1990

Little, Brown and Company

Bulfinch Press / Boston · Toronto · London

Cover: El Capitan, Winter, Sunrise, Yosemite National Park, California, 1968

New Moon

First Quarter

Full Moon

Last Quarter

Copyright © 1989 by the Trustees of The Ansel Adams Publishing Rights Trust.
All rights reserved. No part of this calendar may be reproduced in any form or by any mechanical means, including information storage and retrieval systems, without permission in writing from the publisher.

ISBN 0-8212-1741-0

Bulfinch Press is an imprint and trademark of Little, Brown and Company (Inc.)
Published simultaneously in Canada by Little, Brown & Company (Canada) Limited

Designed by Stephen Harvard
Composition by Meriden-Stinehour Press
Printed by Gardner Lithograph

PRINTED IN THE UNITED STATES OF AMERICA

Ansel Adams

To photograph truthfully and effectively is to see beneath the surfaces and record the qualities of nature and humanity which live or are latent in all things. Impression is not enough. Design, style, technique — these, too, are not enough. Art must reach further than impression or self-revelation. Art, said Alfred Stieglitz, is the affirmation of life. And life, or its eternal evidence, is everywhere.

Some photographers take reality as the sculptors take wood and stone and upon it impose the dominations of their own thought and spirit. Others come before reality more tenderly and a photograph to them is an instrument of love and revelation. A true photograph need not be explained, nor can be contained in words.

—from *The Portfolios of Ansel Adams*,
Portfolio One, 1948

Half Dome, Blowing Snow, Yosemite National Park, California, c. 1955

Merced River and Snow from Columbia Point, Yosemite National Park, California, c. 1923

Grounded Iceberg, Glacier Bay National Monument, Alaska, 1948

Lone Pine Peak, Sierra Nevada, California, c. 1960

Half Dome, Reflections, Merced River, Winter, Yosemite National Park, California, c. 1945

Mount Resplendent, Mount Robson National Park, Canada, 1928

Pine Branch in Snow, Yosemite National Park, c. 1932

The Minarets and Iceberg Lake from Volcanic Ridge, Sierra Nevada, California, c. 1935

Rock and Foam, Tenaya Lake, Yosemite National Park, California, c. 1960

Storm Surf and Rocks, Timber Cove, California, c. 1960

Fern Spring, Dusk, Yosemite National Park, California, c. 1961

El Capitan, Merced River, Clouds, Yosemite National Park, California, c. 1952

Grass and Water, Tuolumne Meadows, Yosemite National Park, California, c. 1935

Grass and Burnt Tree, Sierra Nevada, California, 1935

Oak Tree, Rain, Sonoma County, California, c. 1960

Cottonwood Trunks, Yosemite National Park, California, 1932

Grass in Rain, Glacier Bay National Monument, Alaska, 1948

Lodgepole Pines, Lyell Fork of the Merced River, Yosemite National Park, California, 1921

El Capitan, Sunrise, Yosemite National Park, California, 1956

Tenaya Creek, Dogwood, Rain, Yosemite Valley, c. 1936

Forest, Castle Rock State Park, California, 1962

Rose and Driftwood, San Francisco, California, c. 1932

Bridal Veil Fall, Yosemite National Park, California, c. 1927

El Capitan Fall, Yosemite National Park, California, c. 1940

Base of Upper Yosemite Fall, Yosemite National Park, California, c. 1950

Upper Yosemite Fall, Yosemite National Park, California, c. 1935

Afternoon Sun, Crater Lake National Park, Oregon, 1943

Polemoniums on Mount Gibbs, Sierra Nevada, California, c. 1945

Siesta Lake, Yosemite National Park, California, c. 1958

Tenaya Lake, Mount Conness, Yosemite National Park, California, c. 1946

Refugio Beach, California, 1938

Dune, White Sands National Monument, New Mexico, 1941

Sand Dunes, White Sands National Monument, New Mexico, c. 1942

The White Church, Hornitos, California, 1946

Courthouse, Mariposa, California, c. 1933

Factory Building, San Francisco, California, 1932

White Stump, Sierra Nevada, California, c. 1936

Boards and Thistles, San Francisco, California, 1932

Madrone Bark, Santa Cruz Mountains, California, 1932

Edward Weston, Carmel Highlands, California, 1945

Mount LeConte, Autumn, Great Smoky Mountains National Park, Tennessee, c. 1950

Silverton, Colorado, 1951

Aspen Grove, North Rim, Grand Canyon National Park, Arizona, c. 1947

The Great White Throne, Zion National Park, Utah, 1942

Cape Royal, from South Rim, Grand Canyon National Park, Arizona, c. 1947

Sunrise, Old Walpi Pueblo, Arizona, c. 1942

Winnowing Grain, Taos Pueblo, New Mexico, c. 1929

Monument Valley, Arizona, 1958

Ice on Ellery Lake, Sierra Nevada, California, c. 1959

Summit of El Capitan, Clouds, Yosemite National Park, California, c. 1970

Oak Tree in Snow, Yosemite National Park, California, c. 1933

Sugar Pine Boughs and Lichen, Yosemite National Park, California, 1962

El Capitan, Winter, Sunrise, Yosemite National Park, California, 1968

1990

JANUARY
S	M	T	W	T	F	S
	1	2	3	4	5	6
7	8	9	10	11	12	13
14	15	16	17	18	19	20
21	22	23	24	25	26	27
28	29	30	31			

FEBRUARY
S	M	T	W	T	F	S
				1	2	3
4	5	6	7	8	9	10
11	12	13	14	15	16	17
18	19	20	21	22	23	24
25	26	27	28			

MARCH
S	M	T	W	T	F	S
				1	2	3
4	5	6	7	8	9	10
11	12	13	14	15	16	17
18	19	20	21	22	23	24
25	26	27	28	29	30	31

APRIL
S	M	T	W	T	F	S
1	2	3	4	5	6	7
8	9	10	11	12	13	14
15	16	17	18	19	20	21
22	23	24	25	26	27	28
29	30					

MAY
S	M	T	W	T	F	S
		1	2	3	4	5
6	7	8	9	10	11	12
13	14	15	16	17	18	19
20	21	22	23	24	25	26
27	28	29	30	31		

JUNE
S	M	T	W	T	F	S
					1	2
3	4	5	6	7	8	9
10	11	12	13	14	15	16
17	18	19	20	21	22	23
24	25	26	27	28	29	30

JULY
S	M	T	W	T	F	S
1	2	3	4	5	6	7
8	9	10	11	12	13	14
15	16	17	18	19	20	21
22	23	24	25	26	27	28
29	30	31				

AUGUST
S	M	T	W	T	F	S
			1	2	3	4
5	6	7	8	9	10	11
12	13	14	15	16	17	18
19	20	21	22	23	24	25
26	27	28	29	30	31	

SEPTEMBER
S	M	T	W	T	F	S
						1
2	3	4	5	6	7	8
9	10	11	12	13	14	15
16	17	18	19	20	21	22
23	24	25	26	27	28	29
30						

OCTOBER
S	M	T	W	T	F	S
	1	2	3	4	5	6
7	8	9	10	11	12	13
14	15	16	17	18	19	20
21	22	23	24	25	26	27
28	29	30	31			

NOVEMBER
S	M	T	W	T	F	S
				1	2	3
4	5	6	7	8	9	10
11	12	13	14	15	16	17
18	19	20	21	22	23	24
25	26	27	28	29	30	

DECEMBER
S	M	T	W	T	F	S
						1
2	3	4	5	6	7	8
9	10	11	12	13	14	15
16	17	18	19	20	21	22
23	24	25	26	27	28	29
30	31					

1991

JANUARY
S	M	T	W	T	F	S
		1	2	3	4	5
6	7	8	9	10	11	12
13	14	15	16	17	18	19
20	21	22	23	24	25	26
27	28	29	30	31		

FEBRUARY
S	M	T	W	T	F	S
					1	2
3	4	5	6	7	8	9
10	11	12	13	14	15	16
17	18	19	20	21	22	23
24	25	26	27	28		

MARCH
S	M	T	W	T	F	S
					1	2
3	4	5	6	7	8	9
10	11	12	13	14	15	16
17	18	19	20	21	22	23
24	25	26	27	28	29	30
31						

APRIL
S	M	T	W	T	F	S
	1	2	3	4	5	6
7	8	9	10	11	12	13
14	15	16	17	18	19	20
21	22	23	24	25	26	27
28	29	30				

MAY
S	M	T	W	T	F	S
			1	2	3	4
5	6	7	8	9	10	11
12	13	14	15	16	17	18
19	20	21	22	23	24	25
26	27	28	29	30	31	

JUNE
S	M	T	W	T	F	S
						1
2	3	4	5	6	7	8
9	10	11	12	13	14	15
16	17	18	19	20	21	22
23	24	25	26	27	28	29
30						

JULY
S	M	T	W	T	F	S
	1	2	3	4	5	6
7	8	9	10	11	12	13
14	15	16	17	18	19	20
21	22	23	24	25	26	27
28	29	30	31			

AUGUST
S	M	T	W	T	F	S
				1	2	3
4	5	6	7	8	9	10
11	12	13	14	15	16	17
18	19	20	21	22	23	24
25	26	27	28	29	30	31

SEPTEMBER
S	M	T	W	T	F	S
1	2	3	4	5	6	7
8	9	10	11	12	13	14
15	16	17	18	19	20	21
22	23	24	25	26	27	28
29	30					

OCTOBER
S	M	T	W	T	F	S
		1	2	3	4	5
6	7	8	9	10	11	12
13	14	15	16	17	18	19
20	21	22	23	24	25	26
27	28	29	30	31		

NOVEMBER
S	M	T	W	T	F	S
					1	2
3	4	5	6	7	8	9
10	11	12	13	14	15	16
17	18	19	20	21	22	23
24	25	26	27	28	29	30

DECEMBER
S	M	T	W	T	F	S
1	2	3	4	5	6	7
8	9	10	11	12	13	14
15	16	17	18	19	20	21
22	23	24	25	26	27	28
29	30	31				

Posters by Ansel Adams
The finest quality reproductions on heavy coated paper, suitable for framing

Old Faithful Geyser

Frozen Lake and Cliffs

Aspens (vertical)

Leaves, Mount Rainier

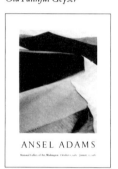
Sand Dunes, Sunrise

Winter Sunrise

Oak Tree, Snowstorm

Clearing Winter Storm

Moon and Half Dome

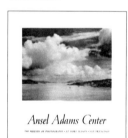
The Golden Gate before the Bridge

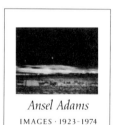
Moonrise, Hernandez

Monolith, The Face of Half Dome

The Tetons and the Snake River

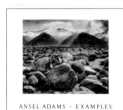
Mount Williamson

Aspens (horizontal)

Mount McKinley and Wonder Lake

El Capitan, Winter, Sunrise

Order Form

Name _____

Address _____

City _____ State _____ Zip _____

QUANTITY		PRICE	TOTAL
	Books by Ansel Adams		
	(All books are hardcover unless otherwise indicated.)		
_____	Ansel Adams: An Autobiography (1596-5)*	$60.00	$_____
_____	Ansel Adams: Classic Images (1629-5)	$29.45	$_____
_____	Ansel Adams: Letters and Images 1916–1984 (1691-0)	$50.00	$_____
_____	Examples: The Making of 40 Photographs (1551-5)	$44.00	$_____
_____	Examples: The Making of 40 Photographs — Paperback (1750-X)	$27.00	$_____
_____	Photographs of the Southwest (0699-0)	$44.00	$_____
_____	Photographs of the Southwest — Paperback (1574-4)	$24.50	$_____
_____	The Portfolios of Ansel Adams (0723-7)	$45.00	$_____
_____	The Portfolios of Ansel Adams — Paperback (1122-6)	$24.50	$_____
_____	Singular Images — Paperback (0728-8)	$14.45	$_____
_____	Yosemite and the Range of Light (0750-4)	$150.00	$_____
_____	Yosemite and the Range of Light — Paperback (1523-X)	$24.50	$_____
	The New Ansel Adams Photography Series		
_____	The Camera / Book 1 (1092-0)	$24.50	$_____
_____	The Negative / Book 2 (1131-5)	$24.50	$_____
_____	The Print / Book 3 (1526-4)	$24.50	$_____
	Posters by Ansel Adams		
_____	Aspens, Northern New Mexico (horizontal) (1742-9)	$25.00	$_____
_____	Aspens, Northern New Mexico (vertical) (1498-5)	$25.00	$_____
_____	Clearing Winter Storm (1496-9)	$25.00	$_____
_____	El Capitan, Winter, Sunrise (1743-7)	$25.00	$_____
_____	Frozen Lake and Cliffs (1532-9)	$25.00	$_____
_____	The Golden Gate before the Bridge (1654-6)	$25.00	$_____

continued overleaf

	Leaves, Mount Rainier (1567-1)*	$25.00	$_____
_____	Monolith, The Face of Half Dome (1531-0)	$25.00	$_____
_____	Moon and Half Dome (1592-2)	$25.00	$_____
_____	Moonrise, Hernandez, New Mexico (1134-X)	$25.00	$_____
_____	Mount McKinley and Wonder Lake (1591-4)	$25.00	$_____
_____	Mount Williamson, Sierra Nevada (1566-3)	$25.00	$_____
_____	Oak Tree, Snowstorm (1568-X)	$25.00	$_____
_____	Old Faithful Geyser (1694-5)	$25.00	$_____
_____	Sand Dunes, Sunrise (1590-6)	$25.00	$_____
_____	The Tetons and the Snake River (1693-7)	$25.00	$_____
_____	Winter Sunrise, Sierra Nevada (1533-7)	$25.00	$_____

Calendars by Ansel Adams

_____	The Ansel Adams 1990 Wall Calendar (1740-2)	$14.95	$_____
_____	The Ansel Adams 1990 Engagement Calendar (1741-0)	$12.95	$_____

Total $_____

Please add $1.50 per item for shipping $_____

Massachusetts, California, and New York residents must include sales tax** $_____

Total $_____

I enclose check/money order payable to Little, Brown and Company for $_____

Charge my ☐ American Express ☐ Visa ☐ MasterCard

Account number ☐☐☐☐ ☐☐☐☐ ☐☐☐☐ ☐☐☐☐

Expiration date _____   Signature _____

MasterCard only—please enter 4-digit number to the left of your name ☐☐☐☐

Ansel Adams books and posters are also available at bookstores.

*ISBN prefix is 0-8212–
**MA—5%; CA—6%; NY—4%; NYC—8.25%
Prices shown on this order form are current prices and are subject to change without notice.

Send all orders to: Little, Brown and Company
Fulfillment Center
200 West Street
P.O. Box 902
Waltham, MA 02254–9961
Or call toll-free: 1–800–992–6947